Sunday Mass Readings

The thinking
behind the Lectionary

by Thomas O'Loughlin
Professor of Historical Theology
University of Nottingham

*All booklets are published thanks to the
generous support of the members of the
Catholic Truth Society*

CATHOLIC TRUTH SOCIETY
PUBLISHERS TO THE HOLY SEE

Contents

A Reading Plan 3

Year A at a glance - The Year of Matthew 17

Year B at a glance - The Year of Mark 24

Year C at a glance - The Year of Luke 30

The Sequence of Second Readings 40

Conclusion 45

Further Reading 48

A Reading Plan

A reading from …

On any Sunday morning millions of Catholics will hear at least four passages from the scriptures. Typically, this will include:

- a passage from a book written before the time of Jesus (e.g. a reading from the Book of Numbers)
- a hymn which may have been composed for the liturgy in the temple in Jerusalem (what we refer to as '*the Responsorial Psalm*')
- a short passage from a letter by the one of the first generation of Christians written to encourage their fellow Christians or explain aspects of discipleship to them (e.g. a reading from the Letter of Paul to the Romans)
- a passage from one of the gospels: this will hold pride of place, it will be listened to standing, begun and ended with music, and sometimes the act of reading will be enhanced with a procession of the book, and then the book will be incensed and flanked with candles.

On any Sunday the same readings will be heard in every Catholic community around the world; and in an increasing number of other Christian communities as well.

What these readings mean is the work of a lifetime; but finding out how these particular readings were chosen for this Sunday is a simpler task. Answering that question is what this booklet is about. Knowing how and why the readings we read were chosen, is also a first step towards having a better appreciation of them.

Readings are not just random

You may have heard such a selection of readings on umpteen occasions, and, indeed, may have been the reader many times. If so, have you ever wondered how they were chosen for that particular Sunday?

The first point to note is this: they have not been randomly chosen by the priest or the preacher. Many people think this would be good idea. So, if there was a very sad story in the news that day, some 'appropriate reading' could be chosen. Likewise, if the day is a lovely summer's day we could have some 'nice reading' – the Beatitudes from Matthew 5 for example – then a simple, short sermon and off we could go and enjoy God's creation! Some priests also have the idea that some of the readings are 'too difficult for ordinary people' and think they could make better choices or improve on the official choice by cutting out readings. While these intentions are praiseworthy, the results are, in the longer term, dismal. Whenever the choice of readings is left to an individual, the resulting choice ends up with a narrow range of texts that reflecting particular likes and dislikes. Our faith comes thorough human channels and has a complex history: the larger the range of readings the better. Our faith is also larger than today, this moment, and this feeling: so we need to access the difficult with the easy, the challenging with the comforting, the hard messages as well as those we like. Moreover, we are not just individuals or a just a group who happens to be in the same place: we are the Church, and each church is part of the whole Body of Christ: and so hearing the same stories, reflecting together on the tradition, helps us to grow as people and as one people who are charged with being the heralds of the Good News to our generation.

So to avoid:

- having a narrow range of favourites
- one person's 'take' on what is important
- manipulating the liturgy to make particular points on specific occasions

  Having the Sunday readings set out for us helps us to:

- access a wider range
- take the rough and the smooth of the traditions together
- access the gospels in the sequence like that in which the evangelists first proclaimed them
- have a link with the whole Church reflecting on the good news

  The book that sets the readings – you may have read from it or have seen it carried in procession – is called a *lectionary*. Our present lectionary appeared in 1969 and is one of the great products of the restoration of the liturgy that was initiated by the Second Vatican Council (1962-5). However, despite being over forty years' old – and gaining new and enthusiastic admirers every year among Christians who are not Catholics – it is probably among the least appreciated and studied book of the entire liturgy.

By now some basic questions should have come into view:

- what exactly is a lectionary
- why was one reading chosen and not another
- do the choices for Sunday after Sunday reveal any underlying plan
- is it worthwhile trying to appreciate this plan
- why do we have readings anyway
- why do we have such strange combinations on some Sundays

These are the questions that this booklet sets out to answer.

What is the lectionary?

The lectionary is the book that presents the contents of the scriptures, those ancient writings that Christians hold in reverence for reading at their assemblies, in such a way that portions of text can be read on particular days, for particular events, or in particular situations. A lectionary could be as simple as a list of references which could then be looked up in a bible, the beginning and end of the appointed passages marked, and then the passage read from there. However, for convenience these portions are better printed out with introductions and conclusions, and then arranged in sequences with the all the readings (Old Testament, psalm, epistle, gospel) for a particular liturgy gathered into one place.

There have been many lectionaries over the last two millennia. Our lectionary was planned in the late 1960s as part of the renewal of the liturgy begun by the Second Vatican Council and was first published in 1969 (a second edition with some additions was then published in 1981). It is one of the most carefully planned lectionaries ever, and presents an enormous range of passages for regular use during the two great seasons of Lent/Easter and Advent/ Christmas, and during the rest of the year. It is this last set of readings for the rest of the year, for those Sundays that go to make up 'Ordinary Time,' that is the focus of this booklet.

Why do we use a lectionary?

Obviously, the simplest way to build a lectionary is to opt for a continuous reading of texts: begin a book one week and read one story or incident, then the next time we assemble, read the next passage. This has the advantage of allowing biblical books to be appreciated whole, and it avoids the ever-present temptation to skip over unpleasant bits. To stop us missing out the bits we do not like, or find difficult, is the basic reason for having formally chosen readings. It also means that on any Sunday, right around the world we are listening together.

Given that the gospels are episodic in structure – meaning that we hear of what Jesus did or said on one day, then later we hear what he did later in the next town – this method of continuous reading is ideally suited to them: read one story/incident today, then move to the next tomorrow or next Sunday. However, given that the liturgical year is fundamental to Christian liturgy – a component of practice already established by the time the Acts of the Apostles was written (roughly around 100 A.D.) – the method of continuous reading cannot hold unrivalled sway. Could one read a parable text on Easter Day just because it was the next reading in a sequence? The very fact that the rudiments of the liturgical year predate the gospels has meant that the nature of the day – for example, if today is the day of Pentecost – determines the reading if there is a reading anywhere in the New Testament that is linked to the day we are celebrating. Therefore, at Christmas we need to hear of Bethlehem; at Easter of the resurrection; and on 6th August of the transfiguration. So in our lectionary we use a combination of:

- continuous reading of the gospels for "Ordinary Time"
- themed readings for the seasons of Lent/Easter and Advent/Christmas
- specific readings the great celebrations which link to the accounts in the gospels to the feasts

The three-year cycle

Although the lectionary has to have a themed element (for Christmas and Easter at the very least), it is still desirable that as wide a range of texts as possible be used in the liturgy. The system worked out to achieve this in our lectionary is complex, elaborate, and on a scale never before attempted in Christian liturgical history. It is this sophistication – at once the inevitable need to blend continuous reading with readings fitted to feasts is recognised – that has made it such an achievement. So on certain days in the year when key moments in the Christ-event are to be celebrated, the readings are the same each and every year: the Passion according to John in the Good Friday Liturgy, is the best example. Then there are the 'themed' choices for Christmas and Easter, and to a lesser extent for Lent and for Advent: but the readings are varied over a cycle of three years for the Sundays and other major feasts.

Outside of the special seasons, **in 'ordinary time' the selection is based on continuous reading of the gospels**. Moreover, **the material is spread over a three-year cycle to give a greater variety of gospel material** than ever before. Each year we read one of the evangelists, Matthew, Mark, and Luke (and we read John during the special seasons with some other passages read alongside Mark.

Reading one gospel per year is a simple device that gives us a three year cycle:

- we read Matthew in year A
- we read Mark (with some passages from John) in year B
- we read Luke in year C

For many of us this now seems so obvious a way of doing things that we forget that it was revolutionary in 1969!

How do we know which year it is?

Which gospel is read in any calendar year is determined by the simple method of dividing the date by three: if the remainder is 1, then it is the first year of the cycle and the gospels for Sundays are taken from Matthew's gospel; if the remainder is 2, then it is the second year and we are reading Mark; and if the date is perfectly divisible, then it is year 3.

Here are some examples:

In the year 2010: 2010÷3=670 'and none over'. Hence it is 'year 3' and we read Luke's gospel.

In the year 2011: 2011÷3=670 and a remainder of 1. Hence it is 'year 1' and we read Matthew's gospel.

In the year 2012: 2012÷3=670 and a remainder of 2. Hence it is 'year 2' and we read Mark's gospel.

What is Ordinary Time?

The phrase 'Ordinary Time' came into existence with the 1969 Missal as a name for the time outside Advent-Christmas and Lent-Easter. The phrase 'ordinary time' is an excellent term to capture a most important aspect of ritual time: that there are differences in stress.

At the heart of any sense of time and ritual, time and religion; or time, calendars and memory is the alternation of *stressed* and *unstressed* time. Stressed time is the special occasion, that which is out of the ordinary, that which is marked aside for particular joyful celebration or for special serious attention. In the modern secular year, such stressed times would be the deadline for sending in tax returns or the annual visit of the auditors, or the 'Cup Final', or the week of a major sporting event. These are times that are not just any day, but known about, prepared for beforehand, and times when normal routine can be set aside. But if there are to be such special times, then there has to be unstressed time. When life becomes a perpetual holiday, you have no holidays!

The ordinary is, by contrast with the special times and notable events, the time when we just get on with the job. It is when there is 'nothing special happening' and when we are acting 'normally.' So if we think of the two great festivals of the liturgy, Easter and Christmas, as the great events, then the time not connected with them is the ordinary time.

How are the readings chosen for Ordinary Time?

The core of each Sunday's readings is **the gospel**. So it is a passage of one the gospels, read passage following passage, that sets the tone of the day.

The First Reading

The first reading was then chosen to fit in with the gospel. Each first reading, and **during Ordinary Time these are always from the Old Testament**, was selected as it in some way fills out the gospel.

The Old Testament reading on a Sunday:

- sometimes provides background to the gospel
- sometimes it supplies in outline something we see in its developed form in the gospel
- sometimes it supplies a contrast to the gospels
- sometimes it has the same message as the gospel showing that God's love does not change

The relationship of the first reading with the gospel varies from Sunday to Sunday, but the basic rule holds good that **we always read the first reading with the gospel in mind**. Reading the first reading and the gospel together is intended to shed more light than reading either on its own.

The Responsorial Psalm

The psalms are ancient hymns that have been used in the liturgy long before the time of the Christ. Jesus himself used them as prayers, and we continue to sing them as Church's song of praise. They form the core of the *Liturgy of the Hours* (sometimes referred to as 'saying the Office' or 'reading the breviary') and these hymns have found their way into every liturgical celebration. At the Sunday Eucharist **the psalm is usually a reflection on the first**

reading or intended to act as a prayer of preparation for the gospel. Sometimes that reflection takes the form of a song of praise for God's goodness – if God's love for us is the theme of the first reading and gospel – and sometimes it takes the form of a prayer of petition or lament, if the first reading and gospel dwell on our needs.

The Second Reading

That leaves the second reading. **It stands on its own and is connected with neither the first reading nor the gospel**. It is always, in Ordinary Time, taken from one of the early Christian letters, usually by St Paul or one of his followers. The passages are read following on from one another each week. But there is a problem here: unconnected with the gospel and the first reading, it comes between them and breaks up the sequence. This location between first reading and psalm on the one hand, and the gospel on the other, is not ideal. However, the alternative was to read the piece from the letter first – but that did not seem right as it meant reading a passage from the time after Jesus, then a passage from before Jesus's time, and then back to after his time again. Another alternative was to omit these early letters altogether, but that did not seem right as they were circulated between the churches in the first decades of Christianity (they are older than any of our gospels) and were read at the very earliest gatherings for the meal of the Eucharist. So it appeared to be too big a break with our past simply to not read them. The end result is that the second reading is intrusive (that is why if there is a need to drop a reading for some good reason, it is this reading that is omitted) and very often people think that all three readings are connected (and when they fail to see any link they think is all 'above them' and give up the effort). In our liturgy, **the reading from the early Christian letter stands alone as a piece of teaching**. Sometimes there will be a common theme between this reading and either the first reading or the gospel, or between all three readings, but when this happens it is simply an accident. Because there is no connection between this reading and the first reading with its psalm, it is best if this stand-alone reading is read by a different reader than the first reading. There is a cycle of excerpts from the early Christian letters that runs over the three years of the lectionary. You can see the whole sequence of these laid out in Chapter 5 of this booklet.

The Gospel

The gospels came into existence through the presence in the early churches of men who could offer the teaching of Jesus within the context of his life and person: the good news was Jesus himself, and not just anything he taught. These people who could bring the person of Jesus back to memory were called The Evangelists. There were many in the churches but four came to have unique authority in that not only was their telling of good news valued above that of others, but the record of their telling *in writing* came to be widely found throughout the churches. Their records in writing of the evangelists' preaching are our four gospels: Matthew, Mark, Luke and John. And reading parts of these writings soon became a standard part of the communities Eucharistic meals: to gather and share the meal of the Lord involved recalling his memory through the work of the evangelists. Hence, the reading from the gospel is at the centre of the 'Liturgy of the Word' on Sundays.

Since each evangelist had a different 'take' on the person, life, and teaching of Jesus it is important that we should hear as much of each of them as possible, despite the fact that this involves apparent repetition and the fact that they do not agree in historical details. We all know that if we hear the accounts of two people of an event, we get a more rounded picture. Therefore, hearing all four accounts of Jesus can give us a more rounded view. This is why we read one gospel per year in a three-year cycle (and read John mainly in the special seasons).

Each Sunday in Ordinary Time we read passages from one of the three gospels (Matthew, Mark, Luke), **more or less in sequence**. In each year we get a different set of insights into who Jesus, the Anointed of the Father, is.

Who is the Christ we are following?

This is the question that inspired each of the evangelists to preach their gospels; and each gospel presents a different 'take' on the question. Each one has his own distinctive view, and each has his unique richness. We tend to blur them all together in our memories, but it is good to remember that four views from different angles are always between than just one or a blur of all four. This is why in the lectionary we devote one year to hearing Matthew's view and way of presenting Jesus to us, then a year to Mark, and then a year to Luke. We do not have a special year for John because we hear much from him in the special times (especially Lent/Easter), and we do have a special section devoted to him in the Year of Mark.

Year A at a glance - The Year of Matthew

The Year of Matthew presents Jesus as the one who, as the Christ, preaches and inaugurated the Kingdom of God. The year is envisaged by the Lectionary as comprising seven units ranging in length from one Sunday (unit VII) to nine Sundays (Unit VI).

The core of the year is the five great 'sermons' that go to make up Matthew's gospel, and these form Units II, III, IV, V, and VI; preceded by Unit I on the figure of Jesus the Christ; and concluded by the last Sunday of the year focusing on the fulfilment of God's kingdom (Unit VII).

In this year each 'unit' is made up of two types of text: some narrative (over one or more Sundays), then some discourse (always over more than one Sunday).

The five sermons are:
- The Sermon on the Mount (Sundays 4-9);
- The Mission Sermon (Sundays 11-13);
- The Parable Sermon (Sundays 15-17);
- The Community Sermon (Sundays 23-24); and
- The Final Sermon (Sundays 32-33).

As with schematic divisions of the gospels it is neater to look at in the abstract, than in terms of actual lections chosen. However, it is worth bearing in mind the lectionary's desire to respect, in so far as it can, the five sermon structure of Matthew, as it often helps us to appreciate the rationale behind making the junctions occur where they do, and the choice of accompanying first reading, which often functions as a lens highlighting a particular aspect of the gospel on a particular Sunday.

Lectionary Unit I

This consists of just two Sundays and focuses on the Figure of Jesus the Messiah.

The question, 'who is the Christ', is then explored with the story of Jesus's baptism (Sunday 1) and the witness of John the Baptist (Sunday 2).

Lectionary Unit II

This unit comprises Sundays 3-9, and its focus is on Christ's design for life in God's Kingdom.

There is one Sunday devoted to narrative: Sunday 3 which highlights the call of the first disciples.

The remaining Sundays' gospels are seen as discourse, which together make up the Sermon on the Mount.

Lectionary Unit III

This unit comprises Sundays 10-13, and its focus is on the spread of God's Kingdom.

There is one Sunday devoted to narrative: Sunday 10 which highlights the call of Levi.

The remaining Sundays' gospels are seen as discourse: the Mission Sermon.

Lectionary Unit IV

This unit comprises Sundays 14-17, and its focus is on the mystery of God's Kingdom.

There is one Sunday devoted to narrative: Sunday 13, whose theme is the revelation to the simple.

The remaining Sundays' gospels are seen as discourse, which together make up the Parable Sermon.

Lectionary Unit V

This unit comprises Sundays 18-24, and its focus is on God's Kingdom on earth – the Church of Christ.

There are five Sundays devoted to narrative:

Sunday 18: the feeding of the five thousand;

Sunday 19: Jesus walking on water;

Sunday 20: the healing/exorcism of the Canaanite woman's daughter;

Sunday 21: Peter's confession of Jesus's identity (and to which the lectionary adds the comment 'the primacy conferred'); and

Sunday 22: discipleship and the prophecy of the passion.

This set of five Sundays has less unity than the other units in this Year's lectionary, and the sequence of three Sundays each with a miracle story poses its own difficulties.

The remaining Sundays' gospels (Sundays 23 and 24) are seen as discourse: the Community Sermon.

Lectionary Unit VI

This unit comprises Sundays 25-33, and the lectionary gives it the title of 'Authority and Invitation – the ministry ends.' However, it has far less unity of theme or focus than the other units.

Seven Sundays are presented as devoted to narrative: Sunday 25-31; then Sundays 32 and 33 are presented as discourse: the final sermon.

However, the narrative section begins with four Sundays on which parables are read (25-28); which are followed by three other elements which are located here, as that is roughly where they fall in Matthew's gospel read continuously.

This unit's structure is an attempt to find a logic in Matthew's Gospel, after the fact; and its rationale of 'narrative followed by discourse' is artificial.

Lectionary Unit VII

The Son of Man coming in glory is King

This unit consists of just one Sunday: Sunday 34, the last Sunday of the Year; and the lectionary describes its focus as 'God's kingdom fulfilled.' The theme of the Sunday is the Matthaean presentation of Jesus as the King in judgment at the end of time.

In this unit all three readings form a thematic unity; indeed in Year A the second reading and gospel supply, together, all the basic imagery that underpins the Feast of Christ the King.

The units can be presented thus:

Year A: The Year of Matthew		
Unit	**Type of Gospel**	**Sunday**
1: The Figure of Jesus the Messiah		1
		2
2: Christ's design for life in God's kingdom	Narrative	3
	Discourse: The Sermon on the Mount	4
		5
		6
		7
		8
		9
3: The Spread of God's Kingdom	Narrative	10
	Discourse: The Mission Sermon	11
		12
		13
4: The Mystery of God's Kingdom	Narrative	14
	Discourse: The Parable Sermon	15
		16
		17
5: God's Kingdom on Earth – The Church of Christ	Narrative	18
	Narrative	19
	Narrative	20
	Narrative	21
	Narrative	22
	Discourse: The Community Sermon	23
		24
6: Authority and invitation – the ministry ends	Narrative	25
	Narrative	26
	Narrative	27
	Narrative	28
	Narrative	29
	Narrative	30
	Narrative	31
	Discourse: The Final Sermon	32
		33
7: God's Kingdom fulfilled		34

The sequence of Gospel Readings: an overview

The purpose of this table is to show at a glance the sweep of readings through Matthew in Year A. We must remember, of course, that this sweep is always interrupted by Easter. It also shows at a glance that there is no sequence in the first readings; each being chosen as having some relationship with the gospel of the day.

Sunday	Gospel	First Reading
Lectionary Unit I		
1 – Baptism	*Mt* 3:13-7	*Is* 42:1-4, 6-7
2	*Jn* 1:29-34	*Is* 49:3, 5-6
Lectionary Unit II		
3	*Mt* 4:12-23	*Is* 8:23 – 9:3
4	*Mt* 5:1-12	*Zp* 2:3; 3:12-13
5	*Mt* 5:13-16	*Is* 58:7-10
6	*Mt* 5:17-37	*Si* 15:15-20
7	*Mt* 5:38-48	*Lv* 19:1-2, 17-18
8	*Mt* 6:24-34	*Is* 49:14-15
9	*Mt* 7:21-27	*Dt* 11:18, 26-28, 32
Lectionary Unit III		
10	*Mt* 9:9-13	*Ho* 6:3-6
11	*Mt* 9:36 – 10:8	*Ex* 19:2-6
12	*Mt* 10:26-33	*Jr* 20:10-13
13	*Mt* 10:37-42	*2 K* 4:8-11, 14-16
Lectionary Unit IV		
14	*Mt* 11:25-30	*Zc* 9:9-10
15	*Mt* 13:1-23	*Is* 55:10-11
16	*Mt* 13:24-43	*Wi* 12:13, 16-19
17	*Mt* 13:44-52	*1 K* 3:5, 7-12

Lectionary Unit V

18	*Mt* 14:13-21	*Is* 55:1-3
19	*Mt* 14:22-33	1 *K* 19:9, 11-13
20	*Mt* 15:21-28	*Is* 56:1, 6-7
21	*Mt* 16:13-20	*Is* 22:19-23
22	*Mt* 16:21-27	*Jr* 20:7-9
23	*Mt* 18:15-20	*Ezk* 33:7-9
24	*Mt* 18:21-35	*Si* 27:30-28:7

Lectionary Unit VI

25	*Mt* 20:1-16	*Is* 55:6-9
26	*Mt* 21:28-32	*Ezk* 18:25-28
27	*Mt* 21:33-43	*Is* 5:1-7
28	*Mt* 22:1-14	*Is* 25:6-10
29	*Mt* 22:15-21	*Is* 45:1, 4-6
30	*Mt* 22:34-40	*Ex* 22:20-26
31	*Mt* 23:1-12	*Ml* 1:14-2:2, 8-10
32	*Mt* 25:1-13	*Ws* 6:12-16
33	*Mt* 25:14-30	*Pv* 31:10-31 (bits)

Lectionary Unit VII

34 – Christ the King	*Mt* 25:31-46	*Ezk* 34:11-12, 15-17

Year B at a glance - The Year of Mark

The creators of the lectionary declared that they saw Mark's 'main interest' as 'the person of Jesus himself.' This is seen as progressively revealed in the text as the journey towards Jerusalem moves forward and based around the climactic question 'who do men say that I am?' (*Mk* 8:29). The lectionary sees Peter's 'You are the Christ' as at 'the heart of Mark's gospel.' In taking this position the lectionary is following the mainstream of contemporary exegetical thinking about Mark today.

The Lectionary also explains the inclusion of the 57 verses from John on Sundays 17-21 as incorporating a single unit from John's, 'the sermon on the "Bread of Life"' which it sees as fitting 'well into [a particular] part of Mark's Gospel, which is concerned with Jesus' revelation of himself and is known as "the Bread section".' And, as dovetailing of texts goes, this is about as neat as anything we might find: on Sunday 14 we have Mark 6:30-34 which is followed in the gospel text (6:35-44) with the feeding miracle of the five loaves and the two fish, which is supplanted in the liturgical reading by the bread/feeding/eating sermon from John.

The Year of Mark is divided in the Lectionary as follows:

Lectionary Unit I

This unit consists of just two Sundays which are seen to open the year/the gospel by focusing on the figure of Jesus the Messiah. This is expressed on the Feast of the Baptism (Sunday 1) with Mark's account; and then the call of Andrew and his companion from John's gospel (Sunday 2). The two events taken together provide the witness from heaven and earth to Jesus being the Promised One.

Lectionary Unit II.I

This unit consists of twenty one Sundays (Sundays 3-23 inclusive) whose overall theme is the Mystery of Jesus being progressively revealed. It is made up of three stages: **I.** *Jesus with the Jewish crowds*, **II.** *Jesus with his disciples* and **III.** *Jesus's manifestation of himself.*

The first stage runs from the third to the ninth Sunday. In these gospels we encounter Jesus around the Sea of Galilee, healing a leper and a paralytic, and answering questions about fasting and the Sabbath.

Lectionary Unit II.II

The second stage of this unit, which is concerned with the Mystery of Jesus being progressively revealed, focuses on Jesus with his disciples.

This stage runs from the tenth to the fourteenth Sunday. In these gospels we encounter Jesus facing serious criticism, preaching parables of the Kingdom, calming the storm, healing, and being rejected at Nazareth.

Lectionary Unit II.III

This stage of the second unit (whose overall theme is the Mystery of Jesus being progressively revealed) focuses on Jesus's manifestation of himself.

This stage is unusual in the lectionary for Ordinary Time in that it is made up of sections from John as well as Mark. It begins with two Sundays (15-16) where Jesus gives the Twelve their mission and then manifests compassion on the crowds. This mention of crowds around Jesus is then the cue for a five-Sunday selection from *Jn* 6 on the Eucharist. The stage then concludes with two more gospel readings from Mark on Sundays 22 and 23.

Lectionary Unit III.I

This unit consists of eleven Sundays (Sundays 24-34 inclusive) whose overall theme is the Mystery of the Son of Man. It is made up of three units: **I.** *The 'Way' of the Son of Man*; **II.** *The final revelation in Jerusalem* and **III.** *The fulfilment of the mystery*.

The first stage runs from the twenty-fourth to the thirtieth Sunday. It opens with Peter's confession of faith and then the narrative that immediately follows in Mark.

Lectionary Unit III.II

This stage consists of three Sundays (Sundays 31-33 inclusive) when we read of the final revelation of the identity of the Son of Man in Jerusalem.

Lectionary Unit III.III

This stage consists of the last Sunday of Ordinary Time, when the Feast of Christ the King is seen as the liturgical celebration of the fulfilment of the mystery of the Son of Man.

Although this is seen as the culmination of the Year of Mark, the end of the year's reflection on the End of the Creation is taken from John.

The units can be presented thus:

Year B: The Year of Mark		
Unit	**Stage**	**Sunday**
1: The Figure of Jesus the Messiah		1
		2
2. The Mystery progressively revealed	1. Jesus with the Jewish Crowds	3
		4
		5
		6
		7
		8
		9
	2. Jesus with his disciples	10
		11
		12
		13
		14
	3. Jesus manifests himself	15
		16
		17
		18
		19
		20
		21
		22
		23

		24
		25
		26
3. The Mystery of the Son of Man	1. The 'Way' of the Son of Man	27
		28
		29
		30
	2. Final revelation in Jerusalem	31
		32
		33
	3. The fulfilment of the mystery	34

The sequence of Gospel Readings: an overview

The purpose of this table is to show at a glance the sweep of readings through Mark and John in Year B. We must remember, of course, that this sweep is always interrupted by Easter. It also shows at a glance that there is no sequence in the first readings; each being chosen as having some relationship with the gospel of the day.

Sunday	Gospel	First Reading
Lectionary Unit I		
1 – Baptism	Mk 1:7-11	*Is* 55:1-11
2	*Jn* 1:35-42	1 *S* 3:3-10, 19
Lectionary Unit II – Stage I		
3	Mk 1:14-20	*Jon* 3:1-5, 10
4	Mk 1:21-8	*Dt* 18:15-20
5	Mk 1:29-39	*Jb* 7:1-4, 6-7
6	Mk 1:40-5	*Lv* 13:1-2, 44-6
7	Mk 2:1-12	*Is* 43:18-9, 21-2, 24-5
8	Mk 2:18-22	*Ho* 2:16-7, 21-2
9	Mk 2:23–3:6	*Dt* 5:12-15

Lectionary Unit II – Stage II		
10	Mk 3:20-35	*Gn* 3:9-15
11	Mk 4:26-34	*Ezk* 17:22-4
12	Mk 4:35-41	*Jb* 38:1, 8-11
13	Mk 5:21-43	*Ws* 1:13-5; 2:23-4
14	Mk 6:1-6	*Ezk* 2:2-5
Lectionary Unit II – Stage III		
15	Mk 6:7-13	*Am* 7:12-5
16	Mk 6:30-4	*Jr* 23:1-6
17	*Jn* 6:1-15	2 *K* 4:42-4
18	*Jn* 6:24-35	*Ex* 16:2-4, 12-15
19	*Jn* 6:41-52	1 *K* 19:4-8
20	*Jn* 6:51-58	*Pr* 9:1-6
21	*Jn* 6:60-69	*Jos* 24:1-2, 15-8
22	Mk 7:1-8, 14-5, 21-23	*Dt* 4:1-2, 6-8
23	Mk 7:31-7	*Is* 35:4-7
Lectionary Unit III – Stage I		
24	Mk 8:27-35	*Is* 50:5-9
25	Mk 9:30-37	*Ws* 2:12, 17-20
26	Mk 9:37-42, 44,46-7	*Nb* 11:25-9
27	Mk 10:2-16	*Gn* 2:18-24
28	Mk 10:17-30	*Ws* 7:7-11
29	Mk 10:35-45	*Is* 53:10-11
30	Mk 10:46-52	*Jr* 31:7-9
Lectionary Unit III – Stage II		
31	Mk 12:28b-34	*Dt* 6:2-6
32	Mk 12:38-44	1 *K* 17:10-16
33	Mk 13:24-32	*Dn* 12:1-3
Lectionary Unit III – Stage III		
34 – Christ the King	*Jn* 18:33b-37	*Dn* 7:13-4

Year C at a glance - The Year of Luke

So what view of the Christ is presented to us in the Year of Luke?

The fundamental lectionary dynamic in this year is the semi-continuous reading of Luke (apart from the infancy narrative [used at Christmas] and the passion narrative [used at Easter]). Luke presents the good news spreading out from obscurity to a group, then to Galilee, then to Jerusalem, and out to the ends of the earth. It is the gradual revelation of Jesus as the guide, healer, and bearer of forgiveness to all humanity.

The Year of Luke is envisaged by the Lectionary as comprising eight units ranging in length from one Sunday (Units V and VIII) to eleven Sundays (Unit IV).

We can see Luke's agenda as broadly geographical and spread over his two works: the Gospel and Acts.

Jesus travels from
Nazareth to Jerusalem
and through death and resurrection to his return to the Father.

The Church travels from
Jerusalem to the Earth's Ends
through suffering and death to glory.

The Lectionary consciously adopts this theme, and Luke's travel narrative (chs 9-19) provides the readings for the core of Ordinary Time: Sundays 13-31. This journey is more chronological in structure than geographical, and, therefore, is well suited to being read sequentially in time, Sunday after Sunday.

This journey is also assumed to parallel the journey of the People of God, both collectively and as individuals for it is the journey through life's sufferings and joys. The Lectionary expects that each Sunday is seen in the light of the larger units (groups of Sundays) and the whole journey theme.

Lectionary Unit I

This consists of just two Sundays and focuses on "The Figure of Jesus the Messiah."

The question, who is the Christ, is then explored with the story of Jesus's baptism (Sunday 1) and the manifestation of his glory at the wedding in Cana (Sunday 2).

Lectionary Unit II

Luke's Programme

The second unit is made up of two Sundays with a common theme – indeed they share a single narrative section of the gospel – which is Luke's programme for the ministry of Jesus.

It consists of Sundays 3 and 4, both of which focus on Jesus's visit to the synagogue in Nazareth. These two

Sundays (with the prologue and Jesus's identification of himself as the one fulfilling the prophecy of Isaiah) set the tone for the year: the Jubilee Year has come and with it a new relationship of righteousness between God and his people and so a new relationship of justice among God's people is called for.

Lectionary Unit III

Galilee

This unit is devoted to Jesus's ministry in Galilee. It runs from Sunday 5 to Sunday 12, and contains seven or eight Sundays depending on whether a particular year has thirty-three or thirty-four Sundays in total. This is probably the least useful unit from the standpoint of preaching or teaching as it always broken up by the period of Lent-Eastertide-Trinity (and in some places Corpus Christi).

Its sections/themes are:

Sunday 5	*The call of the first apostles*
Sunday 6	The sermon on the plain (1)
Sunday 7	The sermon on the plain (2)
Sunday 8	The sermon on the plain (3)
Sunday 9	Curing the centurion's servant
Sunday 10	*The widow at Naim*
Sunday 11	*The woman anoints Jesus's feet*
Sunday 12	Peter's confession of faith

The sections of the gospel referred to in *italics* in this chart are incidents that are only found in Luke's gospel and so are texts that are only heard on these Sundays in the Three-Year Cycle, whereas the Luke's texts on the other Sundays may be verbally very similar to texts met elsewhere in the gospels and consequently read on other Sundays over the three years.

Lectionary Unit IV

Towards Jerusalem

This unit is devoted to the first part of the 'Travel Narrative' and its theme is the qualities Jesus demands of those who follow him.

It runs from Sunday 13 to Sunday 23, and contains eleven Sundays. Its sections/themes are:

Sunday 13	*The journey begins*
Sunday 14	*The mission of the seventy-two*
Sunday 15	*The Good Samaritan*
Sunday 16	*At the meal in the house of Martha and Mary*
Sunday 17	*The friend in need*
Sunday 18	*The parable of the rich fool building barns*
Sunday 19	The need for vigilance
Sunday 20	Jesus brings 'not peace but division'
Sunday 21	Few will be saved
Sunday 22	True humility
Sunday 23	The cost of discipleship

The sections of the gospel referred to in *italics* in this chart are incidents that are only found in Luke's gospel and so are texts that are only preached upon on those Sundays in the Three-Year Cycle, whereas Luke's text on the other Sundays may be verbally very similar to texts met elsewhere in the gospels and consequently read on other Sundays over the three years.

Lectionary Unit V

Pardon and Reconciliation

This unit consists of just one Sunday: Sunday 24. Its focus is on the 'Gospel within the Gospel': Jesus's message of pardon and reconciliation. It is devoted to *Lk* 15 (all but three verses of which are only found in this gospel) and which consists of a string of three parables: (1) the lost coin; (2) the lost sheep; and (3) the prodigal son.

Lectionary Unit VI

Towards Jerusalem, again

This unit is devoted to the second part of the 'travel narrative' and explores the obstacles facing those who follow Jesus.

It runs from Sunday 25 to Sunday 31; its sections/themes are:

Sunday 25	*The unjust steward*
Sunday 26	*The rich man and Lazarus*
Sunday 27	*A lesson on faith and dedication*
Sunday 28	*The ten lepers*
Sunday 29	*The unjust judge*

| Sunday 30 | *The Pharisee and the Tax-collector* |
| Sunday 31 | *Meeting Zacchaeus* |

In many ways this is the most characteristic section of Luke's gospel for none of these sections, stories, incidents are found elsewhere in the gospels.

Lectionary Unit VII

In Jerusalem

This unit is devoted to Jesus's ministry in Jerusalem. It consists of just Sunday 32 and Sunday 33; and it has an eschatological theme running through it.

On Sunday 32 we have the debate about the nature of the resurrection; and then on Sunday 33 we have 'the signs' announcing the End.

Lectionary Unit VIII

The Christ is King

This unit consists of just one Sunday: Sunday 34, the Last Sunday of the Year.

The focus is upon reconciliation and this is expressed through reading the account of the repentant thief from the passion narrative. This story is only found in Luke's gospel.

The units can be presented thus:

Year C: The Year of Luke		
Unit		**Sunday**
1: The Figure of Jesus the Messiah	Baptism of Jesus	1
	Wedding at Cana	2
2: Luke's programme for Jesus's ministry	In Nazareth's synagogue	3
	In Nazareth's synagogue	4
3: The Galilean Ministry	*Calls apostles*	5
	Sermon on the plain	6
	Sermon on the plain	7
	Sermon on the plain	8
	The centurion's servant	9
	The widow at Naim	10
	Jesus' feet anointed	11
	Peter confesses faith	12
4: The first part of the 'travel narrative': the qualities Jesus demands in his followers	*The journey begins*	13
	The seventy-two	14
	The Good Samaritan	15
	Meal at Martha's & Mary's	16
	The friend in need	17
	The rich fool's barns	18
	Need for vigilance	19
	'Not peace but division'	20
	Few will be saved	21
	True humility	22
	The cost of discipleship	23
5: The 'Gospel within the Gospel': Pardon and Reconciliation	*The lost coin* *The lost sheep* *The prodigal son*	24

6: The second part of the 'travel narrative': the obstacles facing those who follow Jesus	*The unjust steward*	25
	Rich man and Lazarus	26
	Faith and dedication	27
	The 10 lepers	28
	The unjust judge	29
	Pharisee and Tax-collector	30
	Meeting Zacchaeus	31
7: The ministry in Jerusalem	Resurrection	32
	'Signs' of the End	33
8: Christ the King: Reconciliation	*The crucified king*	34

It should be clear from this overview that many of the gospels this year present very well known passages (e.g. the Good Samaritan, the Prodigal Son, and the meeting with Zacchaeus) that are only met in Luke's gospel. The great strength of the three-year lectionary is that it allows all these great passages (and similar passages in Matthew and Mark) to each 'have their day' when we can remember them, have them as the basis of a homily, and have a change to let them sink deep into our consciousness.

The sequence of Gospel Readings: an overview

The purpose of this table is to provide the references to the gospels in Luke's year, along with the references to their accompanying first readings. If you want to look up a gospel, then it is a good idea to look up the first reading as well. If you are going to read the first reading, and want to look it up to practice reading it, then it is also a good idea to look up the gospel of the day: reading the gospel usually helps one to see the salient points in the first reading.

Sunday	Gospel	First Reading
Lectionary Unit I		
1 – Baptism	Lk 3:15-6; 21-2	*Is* 40:1-5; 9-11
2	*Jn* 2:1-12	*Is* 62:1-5
Lectionary Unit II		
3	Lk 1:1-4; 4:14-21	*Nh* 8:2-6; 8-10
4	Lk 4:21-30	*Jr* 1:4-5; 17-9
Lectionary Unit III		
5	Lk 5:1-11	*Is* 6:1-8
6	Lk 6:17; 20-26	*Jr* 17:5-8
7	Lk 6:27-38	1 *S* 26:2;7-9; 12-13; 22-23
8	Lk 6:39-45	*Si* 27:4-7
9	Lk 7:1-10	1 *K* 8:41-3
10	Lk 7:11-7	1 *K* 17:17-24
11	Lk 7:36-8:3	2 *S* 12:7-10; 13
12	Lk 9: 18-24	*Zc* 13
Lectionary Unit IV		
13	Lk 9:51-62	1 *K* 19:16; 19-21
14	Lk 10:1-12; 17-20	*Is* 66:10-14
15	Lk 10:25-37	*Dt* 30:10-14
16	Lk 10:38-42	*Gn* 18:1-10
17	Lk 11:1-13	*Gn* 18:20-32
18	Lk 12:13-21	*Qo* 1:2; 2:21-3
19	Lk 12: 32-48	*Ws* 18:6-9
20	Lk 12:49-53	*Je* 38:4-6; 8-10
21	Lk 13:22-30	*Is* 66:18-21

22	Lk 14:1; 7-14	*Qo* 3:17-20; 28-9
23	Lk 14: 25-33	*Ws* 9:13-18
Lectionary Unit V		
24	Lk 15:1-32	*Ex* 32:7-11; 13-4
Lectionary Unit VI		
25	Lk 16:1-13	*Am* 8:4-7
26	Lk 16:19-31	*Am* 6:1; 4-7
27	Lk 17:5-10	*Hab* 1:2-3; 2:2-4
28	Lk 17:11-19	*2 K* 5:14-7
29	Lk 18:1-8	*Ex* 17:8-13
30	Lk 18:9-14	*Si* 35:12-4; 16-9
31	Lk 19:1-10	*Ws* 11:22-12:2
Lectionary Unit VII		
32	Lk 20:27-38	*M* 7:1-2; 9-14
33	Lk 21:5-19	*Ml* 3:19-20
Lectionary Unit VIII		
34 – Christ the King	Lk 23:35-43	*2 S* 5:1-3

The Sequence of Second Readings

The Letter to the Colossians (traditionally attributed to Paul, but in all likelihood the work of one of his early assistants) ends with this little bit of instruction: 'And when this letter has been read among you, have it read also in the church of the Laodiceans; and see that you read also the letter from Laodicea' (*Col* 4:16). Reading letters sent by teachers was an important means by which the early churches developed their understanding of what is meant to be Christians and be part of the Church. They received letters, read them, copied them and sent them on to other churches; and the other churches did likewise. The result was that by the middle of the second century there was a standard collection of early letters that were appealed to as authoritative teaching. Most of this collection is found under the name of Paul (although he did not write all thirteen letters that bear his name: some of them are by his disciples; others were attributed to him because he was the best known letter writer), there were three letters under the name of John, two under the name of Peter, one by James, one by Jude, and one letter, the Letter to the Hebrews, circulated anonymously. Because this reading of a letter has been part of our central weekly gathering since the middle of the first century, we still read passages today.

Each reading has to be seen as a distinct little block of teaching offered for our instruction or for reflection on what it means to be a disciple.

The Second Readings/Epistles in Year A

Sunday	Reading
1 – Baptism	*Ac* 10:34-38
2	1 *Co* 1:1-3
3	1 *Co* 1:10-13, 17
4	1 *Co* 1:26-31
5	1 *Co* 2:1-5
6	1 *Co* 2:6-10
7	1 *Co* 3:16-23
8	1 *Co* 4:1-5
9	*Rm* 3:21-25, 28
10	*Rm* 4:18-25
11	*Rm* 5:6-11
12	*Rm* 5:12-15
13	*Rm* 6:3-4, 8-11
14	*Rm* 8:9, 11-13
15	*Rm* 8:18-23
16	*Rm* 8:26-27
17	*Rm* 8:28-30
18	*Rm* 8:35, 37-39
19	*Rm* 9:1-5
20	*Rm* 11:13-15, 29-32
21	*Rm* 11:33-36
22	*Rm* 12:1-2
23	*Rm* 13:8-10
24	*Rm* 14:7-9
25	*Ph* 1:20-24, 27
26	*Ph* 2:1-11
27	*Ph* 4:6-9

28	*Ph* 4:12-14, 19-20
29	1 *Th* 1:1-5
30	1 *Th* 1:5-10
31	1 *Th* 2:7-9, 13
32	1 *Th* 4:13-18
33	1 *Th* 5:1-6
34 – Christ the King	1 *Co* 15:20-26, 28

Table 2: The Second Readings/Epistles in Year B

Sunday	Reading
1 – Baptism	1 *Jn* 5:1-9
2	1 *Co* 6:13-15, 17-20
3	1 *Co* 7:29-31
4	1 *Co* 7:32-35
5	1 *Co* 9:16-9, 22-3
6	1 *Co* 10:31-11:1
7	2 *Co* 1:18-22
8	2 *Co* 3:1-6
9	2 *Co* 4:6-11
10	2 *Co* 4:13-5:1
11	2 *Co* 5:6-10
12	2 *Co* 5:14-17
13	2 *Co* 8:7, 9, 13-5
14	2 *Co* 12:7-10
15	*Ep* 1:3-14
16	*Ep* 2:13-8
17	*Ep* 4:1-6
18	*Ep* 4:17, 20-4
19	*Ep* 4:30-5:2
20	*Ep* 5:15-20
21	*Ep* 5:21-32
22	*Jm* 1:17-8, 21-2, 27
23	*Jm* 2:1-5
24	*Jm* 2:14-8

25	*Jm* 3:16-4:3
26	*Jm* 5:1-6
27	*Heb* 2:9-11
28	*Heb* 4:12-3
29	*Heb* 4:14-6
30	*Heb* 5:1-6
31	*Heb* 7:23-8
32	*Heb* 9:24-8
33	*Heb* 10:11-4, 18
34 – Christ the King	*Rv* 1:5-8

Table 3: The Second Reading/Epistles in Year C

Sunday	Reading
1 – Baptism	*Ti* 2:11-4; 3:4-7
2	1 *Co* 12:4-11
3	1 *Co* 12:12-30
4	1 *Co* 12: 31-13:13
5	1 *Co* 15:1-11
6	1 *Co* 15:12; 16-20
7	1 *Co* 15:45-49
8	1 *Co* 15:54-8
9	*Ga* 1:1-2; 6-10
10	*Ga* 1:11-9
11	*Ga* 2:16; 19-21
12	*Ga* 3:26-9
13	*Ga* 5:1; 13-8
14	*Ga* 6:14-8
15	*Col* 1:15-20
16	*Col* 1:24-18
17	*Col* 2:12-14
18	*Col* 3:1-5; 9-11
19	*Heb* 11:1-2; 8-19
20	*Heb* 12:1-4

21	*Heb* 12:5-7; 11-3
22	*Heb* 12:18-9; 22-4
23	*Phm* 9-10; 12-17
24	1 *Tm* 1:12-7
25	1 *Tm* 2:1-8
26	1 *Tm* 6:11-6
27	2 *Tm* 1:6-14
28	2 *Tm* 2:8-13
29	2 *Tm* 3:14-4:2
30	2 *Tm* 4:6-8; 16-8
31	2 *Th* 1:11-2:2
32	2 *Th* 2:16-3:5
33	2 *Th* 3:7-12
34 – Christ the King	*Co* 1:11-20

The Lectionary's aim

Spread over three years the creators of the lectionary wanted to give us an overview of St Paul's teaching. However, since we get it in little snippets, week by week, that ideal has not found expression in reality. Very often when you have been reading the second reading you may have felt that it seemed to be just a writing in a blue sky: without context or purpose. A useful way to get a better grip on the particular reading is to look up a larger section of the letter beforehand in a bible: sometimes locating the lectionary's passage in its wider literary context, provides important clues as to what is at the heart of the writer's concern. Then with the fuller understanding yourself, you are in a better position to read the passage in a way that conveys its meaning to the Sunday assembly.

Conclusion

From the very beginning Christians have been gathering each week for the Eucharist. Gathered together and with Christ in their midst (cf. *Mt* 18:20), in union with him we have offered thanks to the Father. At these gatherings they recalled the memory of Jesus by hearing the story of his deeds and teaching. As they celebrated their common identity as disciples, they engaged with the memory of Jesus, whose disciples they were. This continued after those stories became recorded as marks on papyrus and were shared between the churches in books. These books are our gospels, and because the remembering Christ is at the core of our gathering, hence the reading from a gospel is at the heart of our readings.

Readings at the Eucharist

But those early communities believed that he was 'the Christ', the 'Anointed One' of the Father who had risen from death 'in accordance with the scriptures' (cf. 1 *Co* 15:3-4). Hence, to appreciate the Christ we hear of in the gospels we have to read those scriptures. Hence the place of the Old Testament reading. Jesus used the psalms like a prayer book, even cited a psalm on the cross (cf. *Ps* 22:1;

Mk 15:34), and so we have also held them in a special place of reverence in our praise and petition, hence we have a psalm relating to the gospel or first reading.

Those early churches shared letters with one another they had received (cf. *Co* 4:16), and read them at their gatherings for the Eucharist. We have kept up this practice dating back to the time of the apostles; hence, the presence of the second reading.

These readings are not just old tales, they are living memories that can bring us into the presence of God. Here is how this was expressed in the *General Instruction on the Lectionary:*

> That word constantly proclaimed in the liturgy is always a living, active word (see *Heb* 4:2) through the power of the Holy Spirit. It expresses the Father's love that never fails in its effectiveness towards us.

Many translations

Reading through this booklet you may already have come to the conclusion that one of the best ways to appreciate the readings of a particular Sunday, perhaps the passage you are reading to the assembly, is to read it beforehand in its larger setting. Ah! But a problem appears: the translation that is read in most Catholic Churches is that of the Jerusalem Bible dating from 1966, but happen to have a different version or have found a different version in the lectionary on the internet! Rather than seeing this as a problem, see it as an opportunity: no translation gets it right all the time. One translation will help with one sentence, another translation with the next sentence: the more translations you can read, the better feel you will get for the passage. The important thing is to spend the time: you are not simply performing a task, you are proclaiming the word in the Church.

Further Reading

For a more in-depth treatment of the lectionary in book form, see Thomas O'Loughlin, *Explaining the Lectionary for Readers* (Dublin 2008)

The key official document to read is the *General Introduction to the Lectionary*, this can be found in several place on the web: liturgyoffice.org.uk/Resources/Rites/Lectionary.pdf

There is a useful collection of other documents at: catholic-resources.org/Lectionary/Links.htm

There is also an electronic copy of the lectionary, with an American translation, on the web: catholic-resources.org/Lectionary/index.html